that Quilt has a Story

Robyn Ginn
with the collaboration of Alan Ginn

First published in 1994 by Boolarong Publications
With Alan & Robyn Ginn, 7 Fairway Crest, Toowoomba, Q. 4350.
Copyright Robyn & Alan Ginn.

National Library of Australia
Cataloguing-in-Publication data

    Ginn, Robyn, 1945-   .
      That quilt has a story.

      ISBN 0 646 17486 X.

      1. Quilting. 2. Patchwork. I. Ginn, Alan (Alan Maxwell). II.
      Title.

    746.46

BOOLARONG PUBLICATIONS
12 Brookes Street, Bowen Hills, Brisbane, Qld 4006

Phototypesetting by Ocean Graphics Pty Ltd, Gold Coast, Qld.
Printed by Fergies Colour Printers, Brisbane.
Bound by Podlich Enterprises, Brisbane.
Colour Separations by Sphere Colour Graphics, Brisbane.

Preface

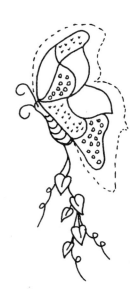

Over the last ten years I have met many people as I have worked with quilters throughout Queensland and, more recently, in Victoria and New South Wales. The working has been fun as many of the quilters have become friends for life. In all of this there has been a recurring question, "We love your quilts, but why do they always have a story?" The simple answer is that I learn ideas and lessons for life best through stories.

Our grandparents and their predecessors seemed to understand that abstract rational instruction was neither the best nor the only way to equip their children for life. They told stories, lots of them, over and over again. Somehow, in our rush through life many of us have lost that art and the belief of its power to teach.

This book is for my children and their children; stories of some of the very simple but valuable lessons for this life, as told through my quilts.

Acknowledgements

Over the last few years, quilters whom I have taught have encouraged me to write down the stories of my quilts. I am indebted to them, as I would not have started without their support.

My husband, Alan, and I have found the preparation of this book to be one of the "interesting experiences" of our lives; I could not do it on my own, I needed his assistance, yet our temperaments are so different. As we worked together and he stretched me to go over my thoughts to put to paper the things that I wanted to say, I was grateful for all the encouragement that I had been given. Without it, I would have given up. My friend, Sue Dalton, has been a great support as she listened each week as we quilted together and I sorted out my thoughts.

Towards the end of our work, some of our friends agreed to review our efforts. They were constructive, (and kind) and I have appreciated their suggestions. With their background in linguistics, Neville and Gwyneth Southwell applied a particularly detailed and analytical approach that was very helpful. We are still friends!

Much of the photography is the result of Michael Stephen's patience as we waited for the "right" day; not too bright, not too dull, not too windy. Not only am I grateful for his technical skills, but his enthusiasm and sense of humour helped enormously in a long and tiring day.

Contents

"Better a handful of quietness than two hands full of
toil and chasing after the wind."

Ecclesiastes 4:6

built the first ship for Captain Cook and had previously signed him on as an apprentice seaman. We laughed at those stories too, because so many of the yarns that he had spun were unbelievable. It was only as an adult that I found that the Captain Cook stories were correct. His stories, their fun and their lessons have stayed with me. I just loved them.

I have a Swedish heritage also. My mother, Sylvia Bengtson, was born of Swedish parents in Australia. In those days every girl became very proficient at sewing and Mum was no exception. She made her school samplers too and eventually graduated to dress-making using her mother's sewing machine. I still have Grandma's sewing machine with all its bits and pieces and her purchase documents as mementos of those times. To complete the picture, my Mum has given me a large number of her school samplers, beautifully presented by sewing on to tissue paper. Many of our young visitors are most intrigued, as they have not seen samplers previously.

Before she married, Mum had purchased her own "Singer" treadle sewing machine. She is now 80 and lives in a retirement village in Bundaberg. Still she sews, and it is not unusual to find her tucked away in her spare room working on her old machine, singing and sewing. It had an electric motor fitted once, but it did not last and has long since been discarded. Mum preferred to use the treadle.

That sewing machine has seen so much work! Mum had produced many embroidered table cloths and linen dressing table sets, as well as her own clothing before she was married. As her children were added to her family, she made all of their clothes; with five children, there were lots of them. That kept her very busy, but she still found time to make hundreds of dresses for missions. So we were raised in an environment which took needle work and machine sewing for granted, as part of a way of life. Of course, my sisters and I were encouraged to sew and to purchase our own sewing machines before marriage.

I had lots of interests as I grew up, and on looking back now I realise that

Mum showed a great deal of patience with me as I took over the dining room table with all my crazes. Stamps, scrap books, sewing, knitting, embroidery and crochet — they all continued up to the time I married.

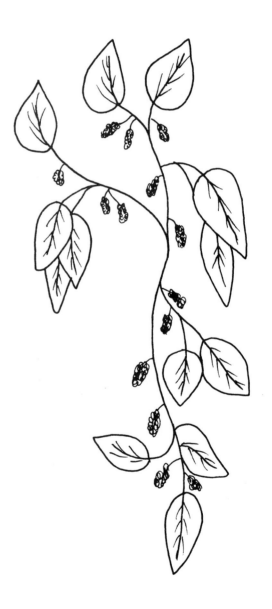

Christmas Stockings
Memories in needlepoint

2

Children, Clothing & Needlepoint

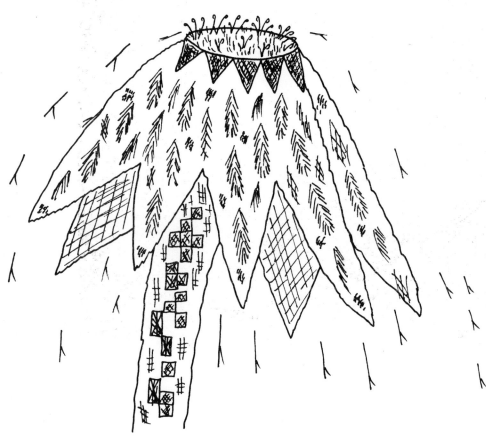

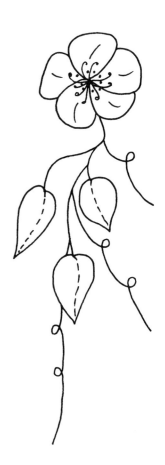

"It's not much use looking ahead,
unless you walk that way."

Anon

Alan and I grew up and went to school in Childers together, though he was a couple of years older than I. I stayed to work there after I left school and Alan went off to Brisbane to study at university. We married after he had finished his first degree and settled in Brisbane. It was not a case of childhood sweethearts, though I must admit that there was some "chemistry" there while we were at school. At first I worked in an office, made my own clothes and just enjoyed my new life.

It was not long before we had three daughters – Fiona, Kylie and Jillian. How life changed! Children's clothing was expensive and limited, so I sewed to save money and also to satisfy my need to be busy creating something.

We lived at Indooroopilly and I bought most of my fabrics and bits and pieces from a little drapery store in the next suburb, at Taringa. Mrs Hughes was the storekeeper and she persuaded me to take up canvas work as a means of achieving relaxation. I became an avoid needlepointer, enjoying the opportunity to work with my hands. At the same time I was able to talk to my three pre-schoolers, to tell them stories and to give them the attention they needed as they entertained themselves at my feet. I had discovered that the children were much happier to watch me sewing than they had been when I attempted to read a book.

My thirst for needlepoint was beyond what we could really afford and, as Alan had an inflated view of my ability, he encouraged me to branch out from commercial tapestries and to design my own canvases. The satisfaction of compiling my own design was very stimulating and the cost saving was enormous. This saving permitted me to indulge my recreation.

I completed dozens of canvases over the next few years, and enjoyed working on each one of them. They now decorate the homes of my family and friends and, of course, my own home. To my friends it was something of a mystery that every project was actually finished and that none finished up in the back of a cupboard somewhere. They probably knew that I am not a particularly patient person, but I had in my ear all the time:

"One thing at a time, and that done well,
Is a very good rule that any can tell."

That saying was given to me by an old lady when I was quite young, in my early teens, I think. As I remember it, she used it as an excuse for not allowing me to interrupt her "one thing", but the message certainly stayed with me; I have become a single project person.

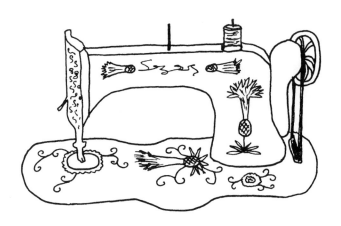

Water Weeds
Freehand to canvas,
Inspired by a playing card

3

Family Time & Sewing Time

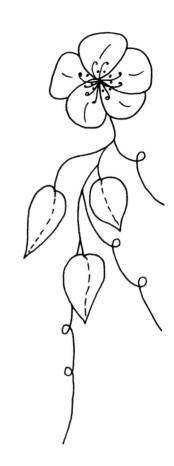

*B*ruce arrived somewhere in the middle of the canvas era. His story would fill a book on its own. We had sought for some time to foster a child and were eventually allocated Bruce. He came as a three-year-old, with the ways of a three-year-old and the life experiences of someone much older. He stayed with us and eventually we were able to adopt him as our son. So I finished up with four children with an age span of five years. I was busy!

Alan was an engineer and he was busy too. He was also addicted to work and would spend many hours after the evening meal reading, writing and planning. Alan's time revolved around activities for work; people and maintenance of home, garden and vehicles; he had no time to call his own. He was not one to sit around and meditate! That sort of relaxation and sleep were to him a waste of time that could be better spent doing more useful things.

We had agreed early in our marriage that we would go to bed at the same time, and then only after we had taken time to talk over the day. So I sat with Alan most nights, sewing, chatting and always "finished my thread". I have sometimes wondered how many thousands of new threads have been started on the way to "finishing my thread". When one is engrossed in a discussion, the new thread seems to start itself automatically! We discussed the activities of the day and shared our thoughts on other things as they came to mind. During those times we worked through the issues that all young families have to face and developed an honest approach to solving our problems.

Tiredness was a problem, but I achieved a great deal and I certainly was never bored. We both feel these late hours were a precious time of our marriage. As a family we faced more than our share of trauma over the next twenty years or so, and we were glad that we had spent so much time together. We did all the things that young families do.

We were involved in the children's schooling and their sport, ballet, music, church work and so on. We created beautiful gardens at three homes over those *years and we enjoyed all of those activities to the full. But when the work was done, the gardening completed and the people had gone home, I went to my chair and took up my needle and thread. It was my recreation, not just my entertainment, and it gave me opportunity to create, to think, to dream and to unwind from the pressures of daily life.*

I always had a project under way and hand sewing had become a way of life for me.

Robyn, sewing and dreaming

4

The First Covers

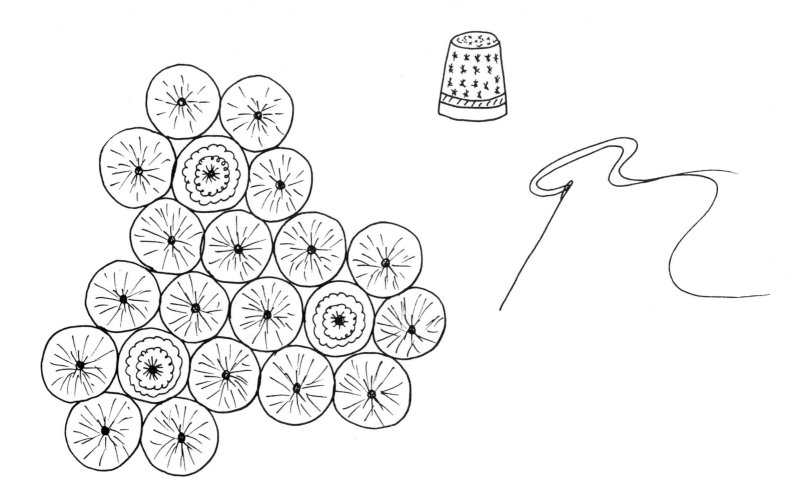

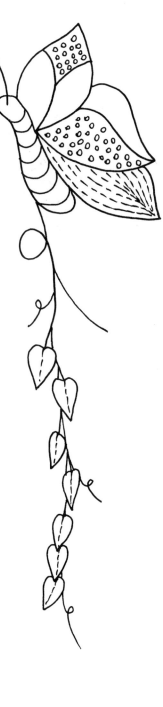

"You can't plow a field by turning
it over in your mind."

Anon

Life was going really well in the mid-seventies. We had four lovely children, a beautiful home, Alan enjoyed his work and I was a happy suburban housewife. Then disaster struck. I lost sensation in my hands and legs and experienced strange tingling feelings when I moved my head. Eventually, it was discovered that I had an unusual upper neck abnormality and surgery was prescribed to try to stabilise it.

The surgeons told me that surgery would be undertaken with my head held in "ice tongs" for traction, and that later I would be encased in a body plaster from the top of my head to my hips for at least three months, perhaps much longer.

I knew that I would have to find something to do with my hands; not for just the three weeks that I was fixed to the "Striker Frame" in hospital, but also for the months of inactivity afterwards at home.

Just weeks before I went to hospital I saw a girl working on a cot quilt made of yo-yo circles. Each piece was smaller and lighter than the canvas work that I had worked on up to that time, so I decided to cut out as many circles as I could to have them ready for hospital.

The nurse who helped me unpack when I arrived in hospital must have wondered what sort of person she had on her hands. There were hundreds of yo-yo circles, needles, threads, a box of new comics (I had to explain that they were for the children during their visits!) and a cassette player with a stack of music tapes.

The hospital experience was traumatic. Not just the surgery, but every few hours the bed was rotated so that I was either flat on my back or flat on my stomach, all

the time with my head in traction. I think that I would have gone insane without my circles and my music.

The bed was no wider than my body, so my arms hung over the sides while I was face down. There was a hole in the bed at face level, so I was able to sew while I lay on my stomach. It was too difficult to sew when I was on my back; my arms became too heavy to hold up for long periods.

Eventually, I was "dressed" in my body cast and allowed to go home. As we were driving down the last painful stretch on the way home from hospital, I suddenly became alert; Alan had just spoken about his intention of buying an Austrian bentwood rocking chair if it proved to be comfortable with the bulk of my plaster cast. Previously, I had begged for one of these (just like my grandmother's), but such extravagance was out of the question. We did purchase a rocker and this was where I sat for most of my waking hours over the next six months until the plaster came off.

The only plus was that it occurred during autumn and winter! It was a most difficult period. The plaster was so heavy and it allowed no activity at all. It was so hard and rigid that I could not cuddle my four small children. Alan banged his nose more than once, causing emotions of both amusement and frustration when he tried to kiss me. We had to laugh sometimes!

My mother came from Childers to help with the chores and to welcome my neighbours and so on. I had never been so still before, and as I sewed away to the sound of music I had lots of time for thinking.

Experiences such as these change you as a person and alter your attitudes to so many things that are taken for granted and followed almost as rituals. In the early days at home I found the prospect of months of sitting in a rocker almost overwhelming and self-pity overcame me.

I knew in my heart that I was fortunate, that one day the plaster would come off and that life would resume. The comfort of God and answered prayer had

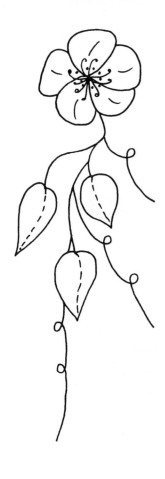

PATCHWORK COVERS

During the school holidays at the end of 1978, I decided to make bed covers for each of my girls. The squares were measured with threads drawn from the fabric and backed but have no batting for softness and warmth. At this stage batting was unknown to me, as I had never seen a quilted quilt.

The fabrics were all given to me by a friend, Erina, who was in the rag trade. The yo-yo quilt had depleted all my own scraps, so the arrival of Erina's fabrics was a wonderful bonus. The covers brought back memories of the covers I had seen as a child.

My head was now almost rigid on my shoulders and I found that I could no longer sew for lengthy periods. It was so stressful making these covers that I have never again sat for so long at a machine.

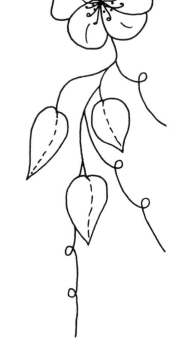

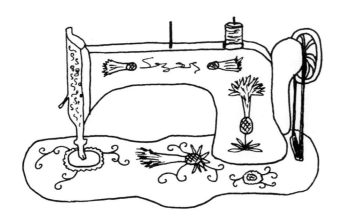

Christmas 1978 A school holiday project
for Fiona, Kylie and Jillian

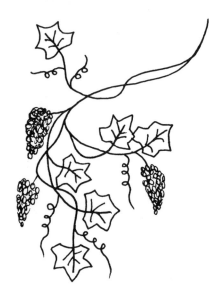

GRAPES

As my canvas work continued, I slowly became more adventurous. I undertook some very large works by cross-stitch and half cross-stitch, but in the end it was my love of embroidery that won out and I started to include embroidery in my canvas work.

The "Grapes" and the "Banksia" are samples of my work during this period and both are worked as woollen embroidery on canvas.

1978 Grapes – Wool on Canvas

LIFE CYCLE of a BANKSIA

Grow in courage in the day of trouble
and you will be strong.

The banksia cones burst open as fires pass through the bush. The fires are essential to the life cycle of the banksia as they cause the seeds to be exposed and released for germination. During the summer rains, the seeds spring into new life and soon a tree develops where the fire swept through.

I like to think of our hardships as initiators of character development. They shake us out of our complacency and bring the realisation that we are vulnerable beings. The summer rains that have caused me to grow are the people who have touched my life and brought both comfort and challenge. They have caused me to think a great deal about the importance of communication and relationships and to act upon my convictions.

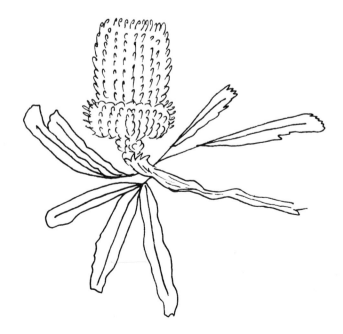

1978 Life Cycle of a Banksia
Wool on Canvas

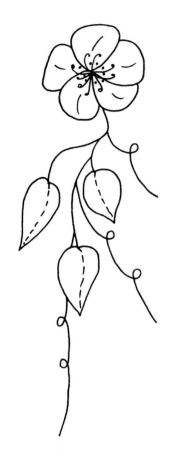

Early in 1979 all of my old symptoms returned. The processes of investigation were as unpleasant as my surgery had been three years before, and they showed that I had to go through it all again. Words cannot describe the emotional conflict that I went through – this time I knew what it was all about before I started.

It was no better the second time around. This time I spent several weeks on a "Rota Bed" packed in sand bags instead of in head traction, before facing another six months in another full body plaster. Again my hands were busy, but this time I chose to crochet woollen rugs. I made three for the family and two for my favourite missionary friends who had retired nearby. Sewing took a long rest.

The surgery revealed that my previous bone graft had not failed and that my skull had broken at the point of contact with the bone graft. The surgeon explained that this was a stress failure, probably caused by some inadvertent movement of my head. His advice was that, as far as possible, I should avoid moving my head downwards or sideways, as these movements placed enormous stress on the bone graft and associated bone structures.

We had anticipated this advice when my problems recurred, and we ordered a specially designed chair to be made while I was in hospital. High arm rests keep my hand work at eye level and the chair rotates so that I do not have to turn my head. For extra comfort over long periods, it also has back and neck supports and is equipped with a rocker mechanism. Since then, this chair has been my place of relaxation for all of my hand sewing.

Quite stringent limits were placed on my activities and I finally realised the seriousness of my neck problems. Previously, I had understood the risk factors of surgery but not the risks associated with even minor physical activity; my lifestyle had to change drastically. I had also observed the strain on Alan and my small children, and so conditioned myself to spend less time on physical activities.

Naturally, my embroidery and canvas work continued, exploring more and

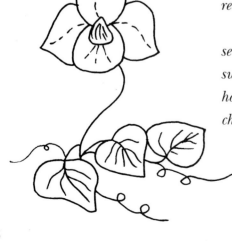

May – November 1979 Following more surgery
"The only way out of something is all the way through it."
An old Chinese Saying

more new stitches and designs. *Eventually, some of my work was included in an exhibition of needlework at the Brisbane City Hall and it was there that I was introduced to the Embroiderers Guild of Queensland. After this I met with a group at the home of Margery Hinton from the Indooroopilly branch of the guild. Instead of exploring my freedom with embroidery, my life opened up to quilts. I was stunned by the beauty of that first quilt!*

I had grown up with scrap covers and eiderdowns but I had never before seen a "real" quilt, i.e., a quilt with batting and quilting stitches to hold the three layers together. I still remember the sadness that I experienced that day as I felt the weight of the quilt and concluded that my neck would not permit me to work with such weight for the time required to complete the project. This group introduced me to hexagons, cathedral windows and all of the other traditional work. As I worked on hexagons I also appliqued squares as gifts within the group. We worked together on a raffle quilt and I enjoyed the talents and generosity of these beautiful women.

I was also frustrated by the thought of going through a procession of designs for the sake of tradition. It just did not appeal to me. In the group there was an American girl who was frustrated by the lack of original Australian designs available to quilters at the time. She encouraged me to create my own designs. The group showed me how a quilt could be broken up into small pieces and worked by the quilt-as-you-go method. That opened all sorts of possibilities for me and so I owe a lot to these women. Their example of sharing time and patterns is one I have sought to follow.

"Difficult things take a long time;
the impossible takes a little longer."
Anon

1982 Hexagon Cloth
set in scallops

5

Applique, Embroidery & Quilting

"Talent grows in peace, character
through the streams of life."
Johann von Goethe

My needlepoint work was put on "hold". It turned out to be a long "hold"; I did not get back to it for more than ten years! Once I had discovered applique work, it did not take long for me to realise that applique would be my real love. The freedom of applique design allowed me to include all my favourite embroidery stitches in my work.

Initially, I wanted to make a hand-worked bed quilt for each of my four children. As the quilts progressed, I found immense satisfaction and became engrossed in the long-term project and in thoughts of the child who was to receive the quilt.

When I think of my imagined happenings, like the pictures I saw in the clouds and my fantasies of riding horses as I gazed over rolling green hills, it is not surprising that I gravitated to "story quilts". Of course, I discovered that reality is quite different. I remember vividly my first horse ride, with a friend and her dad out mustering on a dry brown winter's day. My harmless old horse performed well all day until we turned to head for home. As I clung on for my life, imagining my head hitting against a tree, we pursued this mad race to the home yard. We did not stop until the horse pulled up abruptly in the yard, throwing me to the ground on the other side of the gate. That ground may have been hard, but to me it was safety. The experience did not quite match the fantasy! But then we should not expect it to do so, or much of the adventure of fantasy would be lost.

I have shared my designs and stories with many people over the years. The patterns have been modified and extended many times by talented people to produce beautiful quilts. This gives me great satisfaction and I am pleased to

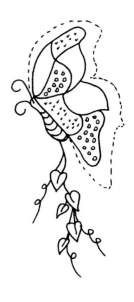

have inspired so many quilters. It is even better to observe the vitality and interest that such work and sharing can bring into women's lives. That is the real reward for me.

This record then is not just about quilts. It is also about dreaming the gifts of life, creativity and beauty that we can derive from our Creator. I am a dreamer who loves to applique, and from that dreaming comes my stories and my designs. Other quilters may surpass me in skill and technique, but my simple designs give me pleasure and the ability to express some of the things I want to say.

The technique of applique can be a limitation in the field of quilting, but I do not find that a difficulty. My applique and embroidery together provide me with sufficient scope to express my creativity and to give me pleasure and satisfaction at the same time.

Doors have opened into the lives of many people during my quilting journey. They have given me encouragement, friendship and learning along the way. My writing is not about techniques – it is about a quilter, her quilts and her dreams.

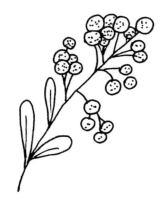

WILDFLOWERS

The "Wildflower" quilts were my first attempt at designing for applique work. I just started, and Alan and the children encouraged me on. By the time I had finished designing I had thirty squares, but the effect of all thirty squares in one quilt was far too overpowering. So the project became two single quilts.

The border for "Wildflowers 1" was purchased while on holiday, on a day trip to Charters Towers in North Queensland. So when I decided to make my project into two quilts, the border material was insufficient for both. The project then became an exercise in the effect of different borders.

A mail order could have been placed with the Charters Towers store, I suppose. However, I remembered walking through rows and rows of fabric piled above my head to find it in the first place and I doubted that my fabric would ever surface again. Years later I was disappointed to see that new management had "spruced up" the store and the charm of the previous treasure hunt was gone.

Wheel of fire	Gum nuts	Iris
Flower garden	Mushrooms	Hibbertia
Wattle	Waterlily	Grevillea
Waratah	Flannel flower	Leptospermum
Wild viola	Wild iris	Cooktown orchid

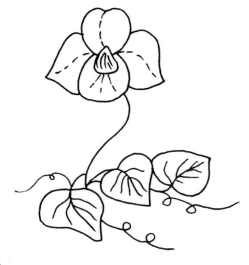

1983 Wildflowers 1
255 cm x 175 cm

WILDFLOWERS 2

"A man's reach shouldn't exceed his grasp."

Anon

Most of these designs were made by folding and cutting the paper to make symmetrical patterns. I attempted to stylise Australian wildflowers and wanted to include hexagons and Dresden plate to symbolise the garden.

My Dresden plate was taken from a traditional pattern, obviously intended for a larger background square. I should not have been surprised, but it was too large, so I turned it into a tree. Alan worked out how much I needed to trim off each piece to make the circle fit, but I found adaptation was an easier way to go. (I never did like maths, and I have no patience with reading instructions!)

Pea family	Bottlebrush	Tree
Macadamia nut	Gum nut	Boronia
Bleeding heart	Hibiscus	Kangaroo paw
Bavera	Paper daisy	Sturt's desert pea
Christmas bells	Geraldton wax	Banksia

1983 Wildflowers 2
255 cm x 175 cm

BACK of "WILDFLOWERS 2"

Both of the "Wildflower" quilts were worked by the quilt-as-you-go method. This is not only less painful for my neck, but it is very suitable for working in the Queensland summer. It can also be used for making a reversible quilt.

Soon after I began these quilts, I met Bonnie Moench. Bonnie had recently arrived from Canada and she was also working by this method of quilting. She became a wonderful encourager and friend. She talked about quilting in North America, where it is common for women to meet in homes and quilt together. Thus Bonnie began our Thursday quilting group. The group still continues, though Bonnie is now in Indonesia and I have moved to Toowoomba.

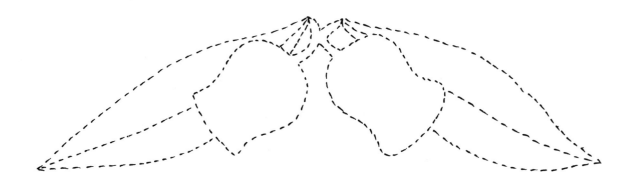

1983 Back of Wildflowers 2
A mix of cottons and poly-cottons

PEACOCK SAMPLER

"A wise youth makes hay while the
sun is shining."

Proverbs 10:5

*T*he four peacocks in the centre of this quilt were first used in "Wildflowers 2"
as a tree. (Remember the failed Dresden plate!) Even while I used the design
as a tree, I knew in my heart that I would later use it as a peacock.

It was fun to repeat each pattern and learn how a change of colour can make
such a difference. Abstract peacocks are quilted in the centre along with lyre birds
in the corners.

1984 Peacock Sampler, for Fiona by hand piecing.
Fiona fell in love with these colours while
they were just a stack of fabrics on the table
240 cm x 200 cm

HEARTS and PUMPKINS

"Faith is a bird that feels dawn breaking;
yet sings while it is still dark."
An old Scandinavian Saying

T he pink colour and theme of hearts and pumpkins suggested romance. Maybe that is why I enjoyed this quilt far more than I expected. Kylie wanted "pink on pink on pink" but she was pleased with the result when I added blue, mustard and mint green. I believed that my enjoyment and creativity should not be stifled by a sixteen-year-old, no matter how much I loved her.

A pumpkin carriage and heart-shaped butterfly are quilted in the centre.

Ruth Stoneley hung this quilt in an exhibition in St John's Cathedral in Brisbane, where it was admired by all romantics. From my early beginnings I remember purchasing fabrics from Ruth's garage and I have appreciated her support and encouragement. Ruth has long been a supporter of quilters and has a genuine love of all quilts, from traditional to original works of art.

1984 Hearts and Pumpkins and thoughts of
Cinderella, for Kylie. Pink was Kylie's favourite
colour when she was 15 and 16
230 cm x 198 cm

JILLIAN'S BUTTERFLY

"Don't give up, it is often the last key
that opens the door."

An old Saying

While I was in a body plaster cast many men made the predictable joke, "If that's what happened to you, what does the other fellow look like?". I was not looking for sympathy, but I found it hard to cope with people who laughed it off as a joke. I learned a new appreciation of people who suffer permanent disabilities. After some time I evolved the reply, "This is my cocoon; one day I'll come out of it and become a butterfly." When the plaster came off, I discovered that nothing much had changed, I was still me and my mirror did not show me a "butterfly". I feel so fortunate that I have been able to throw off my cocoon, but I am often reminded that my body is just the cover that holds the changing, growing "me". A butterfly becomes my symbol.

The butterfly gave me the excuse to use flamboyant colours, and Jill loved them. This quilt has a patch on the back to cover up spots of bleach. We were moving house and Jill had offered to clean down the walls for the much-needed dollar. Alan and I were out when the panic phone call came through. It is fortunate that I always fold my work inside out while I am not working on it. Some quilts continue to accumulate stories, even after they are finished!

What we see is not what we are,
what we are comes from within.

1985 Jillian's Butterfly. Jill loves colour.
Life is never dull when she is around!
240 cm x 200 cm

44

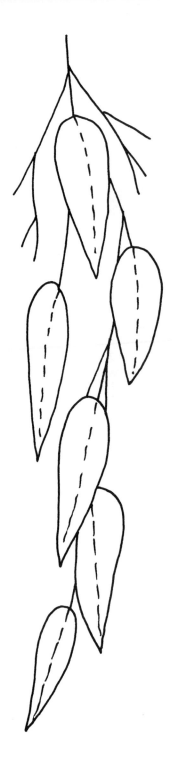

BUSH BABIES 1

And "Woody Pear" was shy and sought
to find a human; but at a distance . . .

I fell in love with May Gibbs' books while reading to my children. I love all the different types of eucalypt nuts and we have gathered quite a collection of them. They are all so different. It is almost as if each one has its own character.

"Woody Pear" (the one in brown with two legs) is most unusual; he is reminiscent of a "dolly" clothes peg and the tree is quite difficult to find in the bush. I can identify with him; he is a little shy, but can be quite an extrovert at times. This quilt is a reminder of the nuts we have collected on many family holidays.

I worked this quilt from fabrics that happened to be in the cupboard, both cottons and poly-cottons, as I talked along with my Mum during one of her visits.

This was the third square that I had worked with the bush baby looking at the sun. Twice before I had worked it as a gift for girls leaving Queensland, "the Sunshine State".

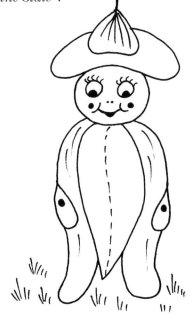

1985 Bush Babies 1
115 cm x 80 cm

46

COUNTRY BIRDS

"The best labour-saving device in use today is tomorrow."

Anon

In 1985 I began to teach hand applique from my home in Kenmore. I was given the courage to do this by Mary and David Rae who had recently arrived from Perth. Mary is a great organiser and she, in effect, presented me with my first class to teach. I had no confidence because I had never been part of a quilting class, I had not taught adults in any formal sense and I knew only one tutor, Ruth Stoneley. So I began by sharing my designs and showing others the techniques for achieving quality work. This strategy has remained the basis of all my teaching work.

My "Country Birds" never became a bed quilt. I was working on this quilt when a "Bush Babies" class persuaded me to teach it to them. After teaching the design and working it through with several students to become a full quilt, I lost the enthusiasm to press on with my own. Students have always seen my work in progress, but after this experience I always finish my project before sharing my patterns.

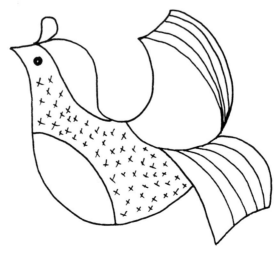

1986 Country Birds
118 cm x 118 cm

48

BUSH BABIES 2

In the freedom of my web, I have
the liberty to move.

T he *"Bush Baby" quilts became favourites with students. They were not only the basis for learning applique work and embroidery stitches, but they also encouraged students to branch out from squares and to develop freedom in design.*

I once had a beginner student who was brought along by her sister. She came rather uncertainly, but she completed a lovely applique quilt in nine blocks of these designs sewn together with stripping. When I admired her work, she confessed that her surgeon husband had sewn the squares together on the machine. She was a beginner who was still able to learn the satisfaction of achievement, and it gave her husband a story to tell!

I encourage my students to treat my patterns as a piano student uses a sheet of music. Not everyone has the ability to write an original score, but many can learn to reproduce that music from it. Some go on to adapt the music and make it their own. By this time they have long forgotten their frustration as they stumbled along with "Baa Baa, black sheep" in their early beginnings. The listener is moved by the beauty of the sound of a competent musician; few people give even a thought to the originality of the music. No-one sits with his hands glued to his lap at the end of a concert, saying, "It was good, but he didn't write it; it's not original." So too, there is beauty and appreciation in contemplating a well-presented completed quilt, irrespective of the originality or otherwise of the design.

1986 Bush Babies 2
Fun with scraps and embroidery
135 cm x 128 cm

SEA . . . SHELLS

"The sea has a boundary assigned to it.
It is told that it can go so far and no
further."

Proverbs 8:29

I had collected fabrics in shell colours and drawn up many shell designs in preparation for this quilt, but in putting designs into fabric I became very bored with the repetition of colour in the apricot appliqued shells. After I had worked the five shells in the centre of the quilt, I explained to my friend, Bonnie, that I was bored with the sameness of colour.

It also troubled me that the shells were too rigid, so I was contemplating the introduction of rocks and waves to bring in some movement. Bonnie was horrified. The rocks, the waves and the story followed. From this I learned that if we only ever work with favourite or limited colours, our quilts have a sameness with only the shape changing, like the shells in the centre of this quilt. This is the reason for the large variety of colours in my work.

Just like the sea, we can be calm and helpful or we can be cyclonic and damaging, but we too have our boundaries. In this quilt I have tried to express the concept of this freedom within borders.

From a poem I once read came the thought that we can "coexist and yet not relate". A wave is slapped in the face as it moves in on a solid rock – to make a move at friendship can be a risk, but it is sometimes very rewarding. We need to be mouldable, not rock hard, and open to those who make "waves" of friendship towards us.

1986 Sea . . . Shells
248 cm x 235 cm

SEA URCHIN

This close-up of the sea urchin highlights the texture created by colonial knots and the freedom of movement that can be achieved with bias strips. I often find myself using both. The other sea urchins are pieced with papers like a Dresden plate.

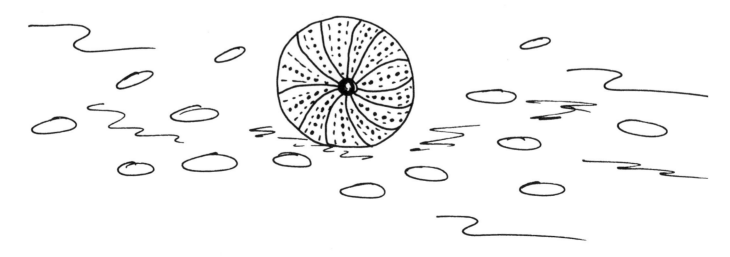

Detail of Sea Urchin

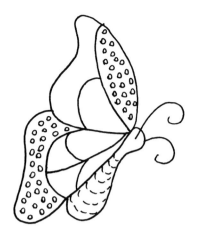

BACK of SEA . . . SHELLS

This quilt was lap quilted in five sections without a hoop. I find this much easier to handle than a full quilt in one piece because of my neck problems. However, the lap quilting requires much closer basting than when quilting on a frame. The basting itself can be an awkward process for many quilters; I certainly found it difficult and usually achieved a migraine headache by the time a quilt had been basted. For more recent quilts, I have really appreciated the ease and quality of basting that can be achieved on an adjustable floor frame.

I no longer quilt square by square, as a well basted quilt makes it possible to handle a large quilt with ease. It also eliminates the effort of joining pieces.

JACKET

Pam Hill was attending applique classes in "Bush Babies" at my home when I described to her the type of V-neck jacket I was wanting to wear for a slim-line effect.

Pam and I worked on the design together. Then, with her sewing and drafting skills and my applique work, we came up with this jacket made from heavy cotton.

This was the beginning of many beautiful jackets of this and similar designs to come out of Queensland.

1986 Jacket, worn by Jillian.

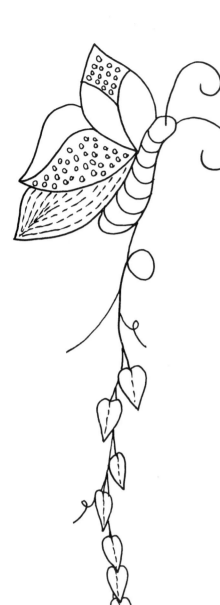

CALICO CAT

"All our talents increase in the using, and every faculty, both good and bad, strengthens by exercise."

Anne Bronte

*D*i Baigent had often talked of my making her a quilt. Eventually, I agreed to work a commission for her, but I did not realise that it would be of a cat. I should have known better. Di loves cats! My designs are all stylised and the idea of a cat frightened me, as it was so different from anything I had ever done. I imagined that she would like a quilt having a realistic image of a cat.

I produced and rejected many sketches and wished I had not agreed to a cat. Finally, I remembered my Mum's blue china cat. It was a gift from one of her children and that memory gave me more to work on than did a realistic cat.

Had I communicated better with Di, I would have saved myself a great deal of frustration. Later, I learned that she liked my work because it was stylised.

1987 Calico Cat
A commission for Di Baigent
161 cm x 130 cm

FREEDOM – ALMOST

"Be strong therefore, and let not your hands be weak: for your work shall be rewarded."

2 Chronicles 15:7

At fifteen, Bruce needed an easy-care quilt. The last thing we needed was tension over a quilt for his use, so I decided on a machine pieced stripe; something small enough to handle on a bed and yet big enough to hide the mess underneath.

For months I had thought about each daughter as I made her quilt and now I felt cheated at the limited thought and effort going into Bruce's one day machine pieced top. It concerned me that Bruce was being cheated also, and that he could later interpret his quilt as a constant reminder that I thought him worthy only of something to hide a mess. As I thought about him and his personality, the kite evolved and was hand appliqued over the top of the stripes.

Bruce has always taken a great deal of effort in constant parenting. In his struggle for freedom, he always seemed to need a restraining hand to assert some control. As Bruce would say goodbye on his way out (to school, or wherever), Alan would always say, "Have a responsible day, son." It was almost dangerous to say, "Have a good day" at that stage of Bruce's life, although, thankfully, things have changed since those days.

As I thought about his life, his quilt became a picture of his struggle for freedom, with my restraining hand loosely holding his string.

1987 Freedom – Almost, for Bruce
207 cm x 133 cm

LETTING GO THE STRING

I made the promise to Bruce when I gave him his quilt that one day I would let go of his string entirely. I promised that, like an eagle teaching its young to fly, I would give him freedom when I knew he was ready. For Bruce, this depended largely on his developing a sense of responsibility and giving his Creator control in his life.

The little kites lost in the clouds are those kids whose parents have "given up" on them.

Jillian's first year of teaching was a difficult year for her. A city girl, she was sent to the country over 1,000 kilometres away. It was a long way from family and friends. The telephone helped us keep in touch with her life and to share in her ups and downs.

On a teaching trip during that year, I visited the central Queensland mining towns a couple of hundred kilometres from her and eventually arrived at her flat. I was so pleased to see her and her home. After the hugs, she began to tell me of a drama in her life and my response offended her; I told her that I was tired of the story and I just wanted the final chapter with the ending. Months later I learned how deeply I had hurt her, and so we talked about the kite.

I have cut the strings and set my children free. In their independence they are bound to have some turbulent moments and may even crash into a tree. I will always be there to listen, to patch up and to help repair them, but I will never again take control of the string.

We are all learning that with freedom comes responsibility, choices and consequences, and sometimes we long for a pilot to take control.

Mum's Hand Letting Go
from Bruce's quilt

64

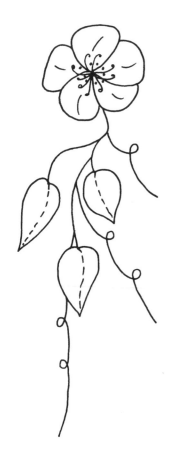

FRIENDSHIP THIMBLES

"A friend is someone who makes
you the centre of attention."

Anon

Friendship quilts bring a mixture of fun and tension. Some are afraid of design while others are concerned that their sewing standard will not find acceptance. Each thimble was to reflect its worker so that I could instantly recognise each friend. I chose the thimble and background fabrics and each member of the group chose the colour she liked to work with.

	Fran		Margaret	
Jan		Margaret		Joan
	Robyn		Bonnie	
Denise		Rhoda		Shirley
	Rosemary		Jackie	

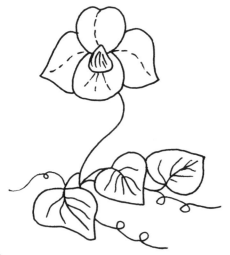

1987 Friendship Thimbles
using some of Grandma's lace
166 cm x 166 cm

66

AND THEN THERE WAS MY GARDEN

Each of my gardens has given me great pleasure as there is always growth and change. As the curtains are opened each morning and I look out into the garden, I love to see the flowers and my soul is nurtured. I have enjoyed many hours in the garden at Bellbowrie, so it is not surprising that a quilt was designed with some of the flowers from that garden.

As the size of a quilt increases, so it becomes more difficult to maintain the intensity of labour that is required for detailed embroidery. The result generally is that the work becomes more stylised. It can also be observed that a great deal of embroidery can become "lost" if applied to a large quilt. In the final analysis, it becomes a matter of effort and reward.

In this quilt, the bias vines and stems provide continuity from one section of the quilt to another. The background of the quilt is light and shadow, symbolising the dappled light that comes to a garden filled with gum trees. There will always be days filled with happiness and days full of shadow, but most days are a mixture of both. This quilt reminds me that there will always be a garden.

1987 And Then There was My Garden
287 cm x 240 cm

70

PUMPKIN CENTRE – QUEENSLAND BLUE

Remember the story of the hungry tramp; he was given a shilling. Eight pence he used to buy bread for his body and the remaining four pence he spent on flowers to feed his soul.

*T*he pumpkin appears out of the compost heap and threatens to take over everything in its path. It speaks to me of food for the body and reminds me that a stable life has balance, feeding both body and soul.

The flowers flowing from squares to rectangles would make this quilt very busy to look at without the resting effect of the larger-than-life pumpkin. Just as the butterfly comes in to rest on a flower, the eyes focus upon the pumpkin.

Pumpkin Centre – Queensland Blue

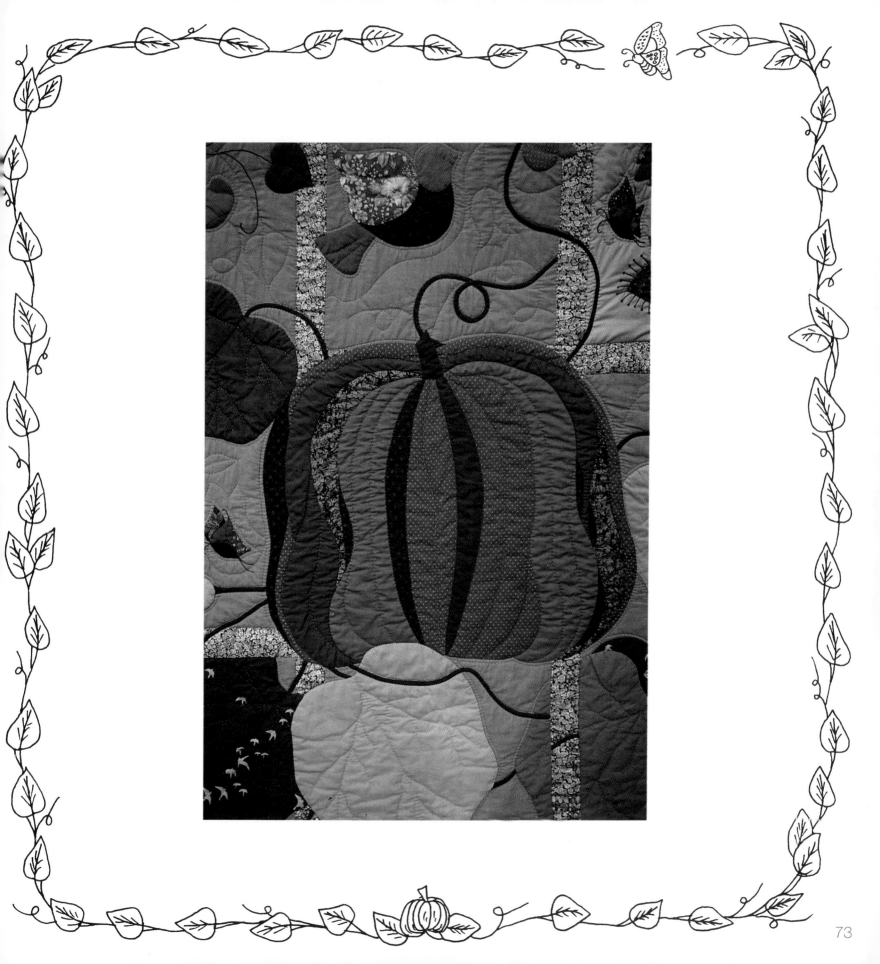

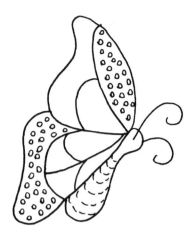

SWEET PEAS

While I was designing this quilt, I was told by a quilting authority that quilt-as-you-go limited quilters to producing medallion and square quilts. I wanted to prove to myself that this was not so, and developed the concept of rectangles and squares for the quilt's background.

One of the advantages of working applique in small sections is that the sections are so convenient and portable. I have seen many unfinished quilts attached to large frames and left in a lonely corner of the house, simply because they are too large and awkward to take for working with a group of friends.

Part of the quilting tradition has been the working of a quilt by a group of women around a large table. The development of the community spirit that accompanies such work is a most important benefit, in my view. This is the common thread that quilters can share. Some of the same benefits can be derived when women meet together to work on their own quilts. It explains why quilting in a group becomes a social bonding experience, not just a sharing of techniques.

OUR BEDROOM AT BELLBOWRIE

This quilt has "Rayfelt" filling and is a wonderfully warm winter quilt. There are some abstract flowers as an excuse for extra colour.

Because my work is stylised and is not intended to represent reality, I am very comfortable with charcoal stems and out-of-proportion design, but it has not always been so. I have always liked to work that way, but have somehow felt that I needed to justify myself for not conforming to the design concepts of traditional quilts.

The pumpkin is not central to the length of the quilt. This provides for the additional length taken up by covering the pillows.

I worked this quilt in sections, with the sides being added last. It has taught me more than any other quilt about the shrinkage that occurs during quilting. Before the final side was added, the unquilted side strip was fifteen centimetres longer than the length of the completed central section.

QUEENSLAND BLUE

This pumpkin is one of a series worked in a hoop for "Quilt Experience". "Quilt Experience" provides live-in workshops over four days and has been held at Minden for six years, Toowoomba for one year, Atherton for two years and Townsville for two years. I have been with "Quilt Experience" as a tutor for all of these except the last one at Townsville when other commitments prevented me.

Sharon Waite and Jan Knight have worked tirelessly to bring live-in quilting workshops to Queensland women at an affordable cost. It is wonderful to be a small part of these events and to see so many creative women together. The learning of techniques is an important part of the event and, indeed, the reason for its existence, but it is not the only attraction.

It has been an experience to share with quilting friends. The friends in quilting are more important to me than the quilts that just happen along the way. Life would be very empty if my only companions were the quilts spilling out of my room.

MORNING GLORY

"It's better to give than to receive,
but receiving isn't bad."

Anon

Some of my friends tell me that I am lucky that my efforts to grow morning glory have been so unsuccessful, and that I should continue to admire it on my walls. I am told that it is a nuisance and that there are no food benefits such as those that come with the take-over of the pumpkin. (So what is wrong with decoration? I still think that the flowers are beautiful!)

This pattern is from my garden quilt. The original "Morning Glory" hoop went to Jakarta with Bonnie Moench when she left Australia. She had long admired my hoop hanging in the kitchen and when I made her a copy as a gift, I found out that the original one was more to her colour blue than was my copy for her – the photograph is of the second one.

Recently Bonnie and I exchanged gifts after an arrangement that we made by telephone. I received a double wedding ring quilt that is made in wonderful dark colours and beautifully quilted. Bonnie chose, in exchange, to have a blue crazy patch teddy bear with embroidery, old buttons and lace. We both feel we did rather well with our "memory exchange", but we do miss our quilting days together.

1987 Morning Glory
A hoop for "Quilt Experience"

PUMPKIN, HEARTS AND BUTTERFLIES

from Kylie's quilt

H*oops make a lovely gift. They do not have to be stuffed, zipped or filled and they look great on a wall.*

"The test of a first-rate work, and a test of
your sincerity in calling it a first-rate work,
is that you finish it."

Arnold Bennett

1987 Pumpkin, Hearts and Butterflies
A hoop for "Quilt Experience"

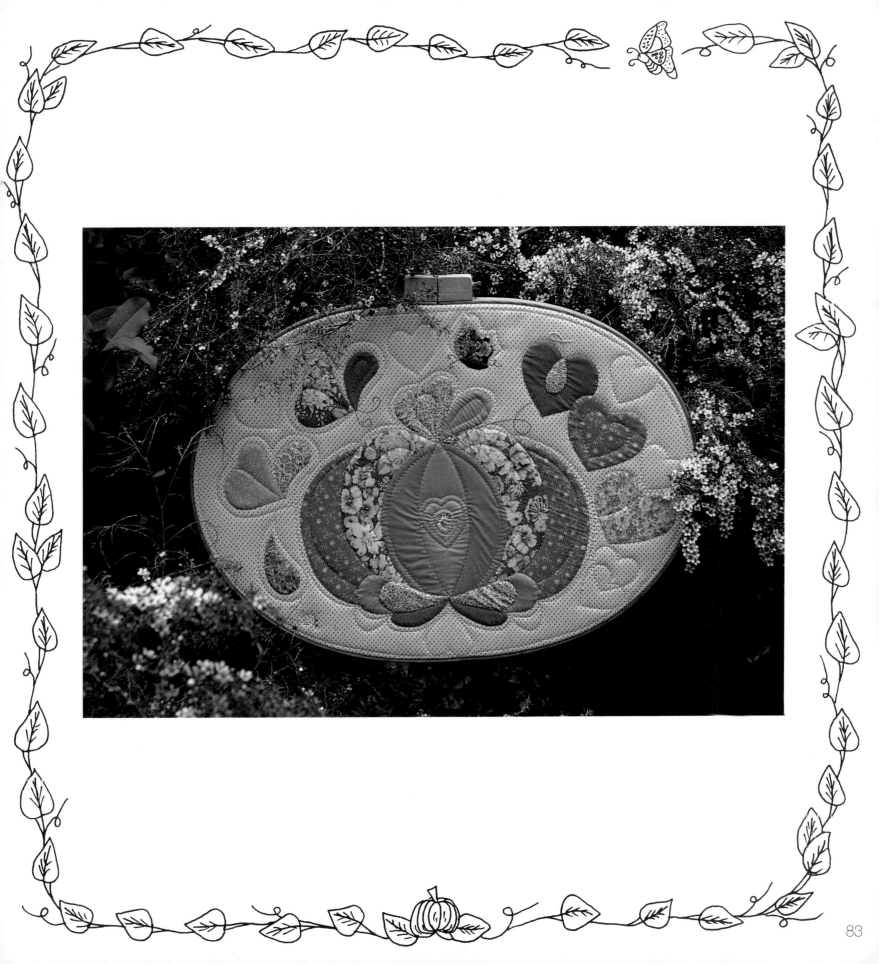

BUTTERFLY

"My way is to begin with the beginning."

Lord Byron

Hoops are useful for a two-day workshop. They give the beginner an early sense of achievement and provide an opportunity for discovering if applique is a technique that she finds enjoyable.

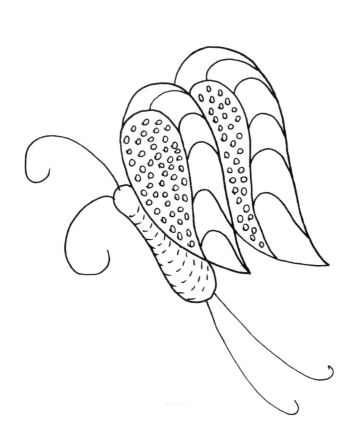

1987 Butterfly
A hoop for "Quilt Experience"
with an exercise in applique.

HE LOVES ME, HE LOVES ME NOT

We once pulled petals off flowers out in the paddock and played, "He loves me, he loves me not", thinking of boyfriends. Some of us now play the game, thinking of our Creator.

In this quilt we are the flowers in cycle, falling from peaks to despair. We have our "up" days and our "down" days, assuming that when we are good, He loves us and that when we are bad, He loves us not. When we are "together", He loves us and when we are breaking apart, He loves us not. The half sunflower reflects the Creator constantly shining down on us. He remains the same, regardless of how we feel, but we are the flowers and are continually changing. Depending on our circumstances and how we feel, we pull off petals and, sadly, our confidence in God can depend on which petal we end up with.

This quilt again shows the balance that we need for harmony. The quilted rays provide the necessary warmth and the quilted rain drops represent the moisture that is so essential for survival and growth.

1988 He Loves Me, He Loves Me Not
Hand pieced and hand quilted
210 cm x 135 cm

A FEW OF MY FAVOURITE THINGS

*G*irls, *birds, houses, gardens and love as well as silk and old lace are some of the things that I like to think about. Having sketched the profile of the lady, I was told that she looks like Kylie, so this wall hanging eventually became hers.*

This lady has now been adapted and used by many students to decorate their homes.

The wall hanging brings back memories of the happy times visiting my grandmother on her property at River Heads near Hervey Bay. If I was very good, she allowed me to play with a china doll that had a face much like the lady in the hanging. She had cattle, goats and chooks and a huge orchard where my older sister and I had many hours of fun. She also had the first cottage garden that I had seen; it was lovely and was fenced off in front of her house to keep the animals out.

1988 A Few of My Favourite Things
In silk and using some of my Grandma's lace
106 cm x 94 cm

MY BRISBANE THURSDAY QUILTERS

"This above all: to thine own self be true."

Shakespeare

*A*nother *"friendship quilt". These girls were given my design of their initial, but with it the option to design their own if they chose.*

Alda	*Sandra*	*Di*
Barb	*Robyn*	*Sue*
Cosette	*Jan*	*Elaine*

When I left Brisbane in 1992, the Thursday group that began with Bonnie was still going. It is a social quilting group of women who have shared their lives and have been supportive of each other.

1988 My
Brisbane
Thursday
Quilters
190 cm x
190 cm

A WATER DROP

*"Can Wisdom be put in a silver rod,
or Love in a golden bowl?"*
William Blake

A lan's career was in the water industry and his last position was that of manager of Brisbane's water and sewerage authority. So I should not have been surprised that his choice for a quilted hanging for his office was inspired by a CSIRO photograph of a drop of water landing on a water surface and then rebounding.

The glass tear drops were to depict water. Little did we know what lay ahead. After many years of cortisone treatment for a severe asthma condition, Alan had to give up his engineering for early retirement.

Long ago, Fiona said to Alan that if he could ask God for one thing, what would it be? Expecting to hear, "Good health", he surprised her by saying "Wisdom". Fiona's reply was, "You know, Dad, that 'with wisdom comes much sorrow'."

It was a wise decision when he was so young to give up work to prolong his life, but it has not been without its sorrow! Life has given us many examples where knowledge and wisdom have given pain and sorrow in putting decisions into practice.

There is a bright side too, of course. Once the decision to retire was made, we have found that retirement need not be the stressful experience that many of my friends predicted that it would be. It is a great advantage that we enjoy each other's company and that we share some interests. We have also maintained our separate interests, and I think that it has been a real plus for us that we still have a home large enough to accommodate these interests without getting in each other's way.

1989 A Water Drop for Alan's office
77 cm x 101 cm

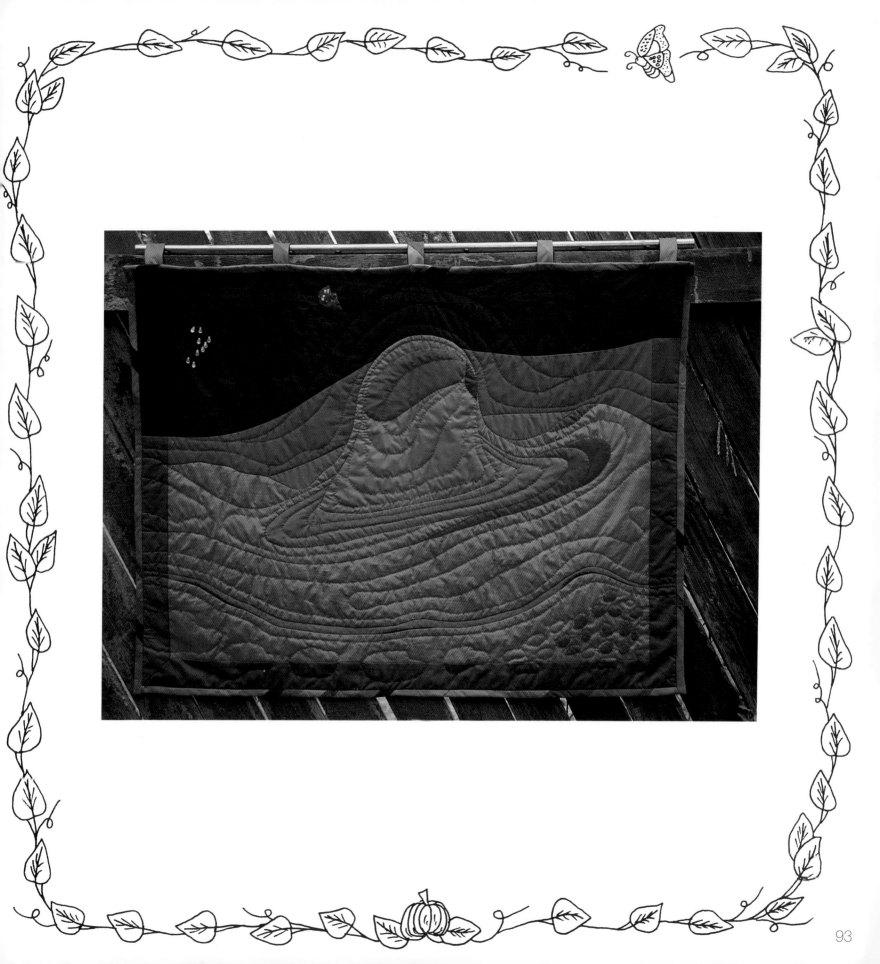

THE YEAR of the TEDDIES

"God Almighty first planted a Garden.
And indeed, it is the purest of human
Pleasures."

Francis Bacon

This patch of the garden was lovely; "He's the lily of the valley . . . In trouble, He's my comfort."

When my four teenagers were too noisy, I would escape down here and renew my strength in the quiet solitude. The garden has always been another love, and under stress I often walk outside to pick up a garden hose and soothe away my cares. It clears away the cobwebs from my mind and helps to keep things in perspective.

Our garden was a setting for many weddings and parties; it was a haven that people enjoyed. I do miss having bunches of arum lilies to fill the home and to share around with friends. Life, however, is about living in the present too and that gives me an abundance of treasures and experiences to be happy about.

Sometime during 1989, a couple of friends persuaded me to go to Caloundra on the Sunshine Coast where a group of quilters was spending the day making crazy patchwork teddy bears. I had a bag of fabrics with me, but I went not expecting to be tempted. Teddies have never interested me and I must have been the only person without a sewing machine. Someone was kind enough to share her machine with me and, by the end of the day, Joan McKenzie and I were the only ones (as I remember it) who had our pieces covered in patches and ready for embroidery. Sewing machines have a "pressure to finish" effect on me! I loved the embroidery, lace, buttons and beads that followed.

1989-1991 The Year of the Teddies
Noffie is a very possessive silky
terrier, so she had to be in Michael's photo
with the teddies.

Once the bear was finished, Steve (Fiona's fiance at the time) begged me to make him a Panda bear, declaring that I could change the pattern and then moaning when I said that it was too hard. I "caved in" to his forlorn looks; it must have been because Fiona was in Alice Springs nursing at the time.

I altered the pattern and Steve traced it on to calico for me. It was the first of many bears that I would make to my adapted pattern. Bears make a fun workshop and I love discovering new ways to use stitches, as tutor and students sit around together.

FANTASY – A DREAMING

Because I am a dreamer, I have a strong bias towards nursery quilts, even though they are no longer practical for my adult children. This quilt's little boy is dreaming of fairies and exciting adventures, but some dreams are locked up in the pumpkin. On the door of the pumpkin I have sewn a gold locket given to me by a special friend, Chrissa.

Steve, my son-in-law, says that the little boy is not just dreaming, "He's overdosed, he's on a trip!" Steve has added spice and flavour to our family; I can rely on him to show us a different perception on many things.

1990 Fantasy – A Dreaming
Appliqued in three sections, quilted as one.
206 cm x 121 cm

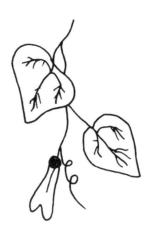

FANTASY – A DREAMING, CLOSE UP

*K*en Medema is a blind singer from the United States. His music has brought me lots of inspiration and pleasure over the years since I first met him. He sings about being told when he was a boy that day-dreaming was a waste of time. As an adult, he encourages people to "come dreaming with me, admission is free". A world without dreams is not a place where we would wish to be.

I know that Ken could tell stories about being rejected by people who are "hard rocks". I have found it fascinating to watch him; all of his approaches towards people need to include physical contact and the risk of rejection. His life experience has made him a very sensitive person, and this comes out in his music.

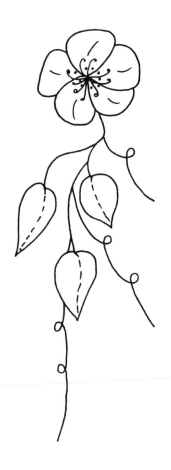

GLIMPSES OF MY PAST – THE CENTRE

The first home that I can remember was an old "Queenslander". These were the traditional homes on stilts, made of timber and lined internally with vertical V-J boards. A feature of these homes was often the "stove recess" – a construction protruding outside the house in which the wood-burning stove was placed. It was usually made of galvanised iron sheeting and a mantel shelf was fixed above the entrance to the stove recess. A decorative frill in fabric, lace or paper was often attached to the mantel shelf.

These are strong memories for me and parts of it can be seen in this quilt. The arch symbolises the warmth of the home. Grandma's jug is above the mantel shelf and scripture is below it, and the quilting is in double stripe like the V-J boards. Scripture verse was always hung on our wall and the one that I have chosen is:

"The grass withers, the flowers fade,
but the word of our God shall stand
forever."

Isaiah 40.8

The border colours deliberately fade a little from top to bottom to reflect the verse.

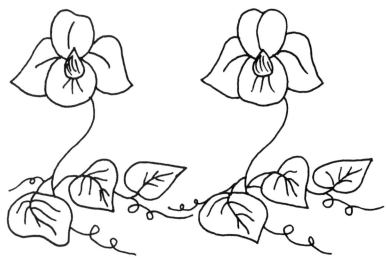

QUILTED SIDES ADDED TO QUILTED CENTRE

If a task is worth doing,
it is worth finishing.

While this quilt was in progress, Alan and I were away from home for a few days staying with some non-quilters. Two dogs entered the house, got into my basket and took off with three completed panels. They destroyed one panel and damaged the other two. The roosters and strawberries had to be re-worked onto new backing. Damage to the sides was minor and was covered by rearranging and replacing leaves.

When we discovered what the dogs had done, I was devastated and struggled to control my thinking. No one, apart from Alan, showed any understanding or sympathy and this compounded the misery that I was feeling. My anger was directed away from the dogs and on to the people. I knew that it was only a quilt, but all of my internal lecturing could not stop the hurt I felt. One of our family sayings, "people matter more than things", helped me gain control of my feelings. Only Alan showed sympathy and an awareness of my struggle as the night of socialising continued.

I felt that I had managed rather well, but as I fell off to sleep I knew that I was wounded by those who could brush off my misfortune with a laugh. I knew that it would take time for me to forgive them. During the night I woke myself crying and was reminded again that I am just "flesh and blood". It was nice to cry in private, and I learned that having control of my emotions in a situation does not prevent the inner turmoil that needs to be dealt with.

The following day I was glad to be with Alan at my brother's home, but I could not face looking at the damage. After several days, Alan and my sister-in-law

persuaded me to inspect the damaged area. With their support, I was able to forgive the lack of sympathy and to start again; forgiveness is such an important part of the healing process.

Stan Nickerson is a friend of ours. He talks of a clean slate as being a picture of God's forgiveness; there is no trace of wrong-doing. By contrast, when we forgive, it is like the scratched-out ink copy books from our childhood; the hole in the paper is a permanent reminder of the mistake.

It was this thought that finally decided me not to patch up the damaged panel of my quilt, but to begin again. I wanted to be reminded of God's love and forgiveness, and not of my scratched-out mistakes.

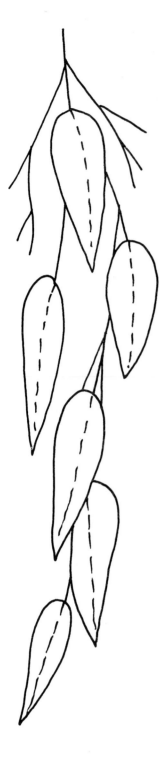

THE RED HEN

A man's generosity is measured not
by the amount of his giving, but by
what he withholds.

My hen reminds me of the simple story in which Hennie Penny's world was falling apart because an acorn had landed on her head. It is a reminder to me not to become unduly upset over trivial matters or mishaps.

I am reminded also of the wise little red hen who planted the wheat to feed the hungry with bread. In her wisdom, she knew that the few grains of wheat would multiply if planted, and would provide flour for many loaves of bread.

Another hen story from which I often take a lesson is the story of the hen and the pig who shared the farmyard. The farm was in drought and the hen became disturbed by the sight of the farmer's hungry children. The hen had an idea; she said to the pig, "I will give my eggs, and you must give your bacon." The pig agreed, but he said, "Remember, for you it is only a token, but for me it is total sacrifice."

Sometimes, we act as if we are afraid to give of ourselves, as if we believe that generosity of spirit will require all of our energy and that nothing will remain – a "total sacrifice". I find it helpful to remember to give my egg each day and still believe that there will be a new supply for the next day.

1991 The Red Hen
81 cm x 93 cm

THE PRODIGAL'S PATH

*"Men's natures are alike; it is their
habits that carry them far apart."*
Confucius

The tree for this hanging was drawn up years earlier, so that when Susie gave me some dyed fabrics I knew where I would use them.

As parents, Alan and I have always encouraged openness of communication within our family. The colours of this quilt hint at the tension this sometimes causes in relationships. As a matter of principle, we also work to ensure that we do not let the sun set on our anger and to ensure that communication is restored. The path is part of the process of restoration; we all experience times when we find eye contact difficult after a tense experience. It reminds us that if we see that person on the way back to us, we can achieve wonders if we make it easier by running down the path to meet them, and thereby achieve reconciliation.

1991 The Prodigal's Path
96 cm x 72 cm

WHAT IS FREEDOM?

> "Everything has its beauty but not everyone sees it."
>
> Confucius

To be free is such a common dream, but the dreams are different for each one of us. For many, it is simply to leave the boredom of a steady life and to search for excitement and the freedom to "do their own thing". So it is no surprise that this horse escaped the carousel; he was tired of having people on his back all day and of going round and round in the same old routine! He left in search of independence, freedom and happiness.

His problem was that he had merely escaped — he had not thought through what he had wanted to be and to do, as an alternative to his carousel existence.

So many of us try to do the same thing in many different ways, but there will be no happiness without achievement and no achievement without other people.

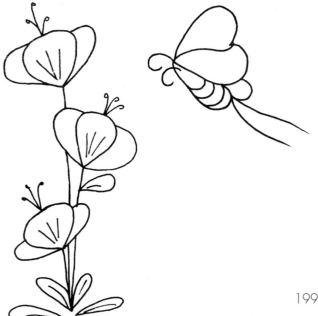

1991 What is Freedom?
273 cm x 225 cm

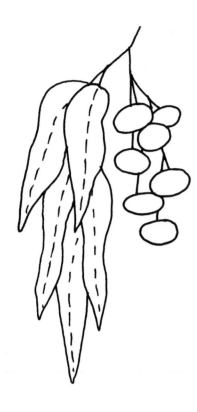

GREEN AND CREAM

I was part way through working my "Wild Berries" quilt when I began this commission for Shelley. I could not cope with working on both quilts at once, so "Wild Berries" was placed to one side until Shelly's quilt was completed.

Shelley's only instruction was for a green and cream quilt suitable for a queen sized bed.

The flowers on the border appear on three of my quilts. These flowers are thunbergia; the white variety grew prolifically over the entrance to our home at Bellbowrie. The dark green leaves were added, hoping to be able to persuade Shelley that the touch of their rust-coloured berries would add interest to the green and cream design. A mix of huge flowers, tiny butterflies, large and small berries and large and small leaves gives an effect that I enjoy in design.

I found the border fabric at Ruth Stoneley's shop after the applique work was almost completed, and it had just the effect that I needed to bring it all together.

Repetition on such a scale is difficult for me, but it does remind me that:

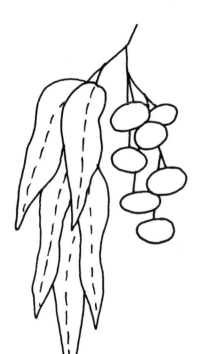

> If we sow with effort,
> we will reap excellence.

In our hearts we know this to be the case in many areas of life. Sometimes, we use little effort, knowing that the result will not be our best.

When I was a child, my mother would say to me, "Robyn, aren't you scared? Don't you know that 'you will reap what you sow'? You are so naughty; it should scare you that you'll have naughty children." One day my back answer flew, "You must have been wicked, because you got me!" In time, I learned the positive side of her scripture quotation; it is no longer a threat to me. Instead, I have observed people, such as the late Professor Fred Hollows, who are fine examples of humanity; compassionate, upright, generous people who have invested effort into putting their beliefs into action. The results are evident for all to see.

1992 Green and Cream
A commission for Shelley
260 cm x 233 cm

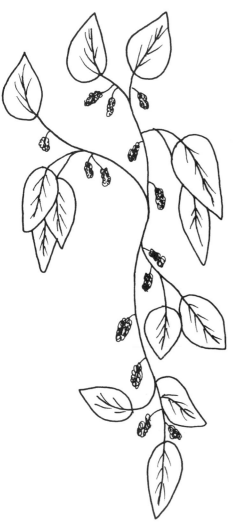

WILD BERRIES

"Love does not consist in gazing at each other
but in looking together in the same direction."
Antoine de Saint-Exupery

This quilt reminds me of all of my quilting friends. The blackberries are those who like the freedom to "do their own thing"; they need very little assistance from a tutor. They may be a bit prickly, yet they make something out of what others would regard as a tangled mess.

Most quilters, however, are like blueberries; they are traditional, structured, unadventurous, tidy and stray only slightly from their original inspiration.

Some quilters are like lillypillys, beautiful to look at. Few would dare to pick them, as they are bitter to taste. They are those who are not generous with their abundance.

A few, like ardisseas, have people flocking around their beauty, but they are not edible at all. Every group needs the entertainment they provide, even though they may not be at all productive on the day.

Then there are the mulberries, lovely and tasty, but they make an awful mess when you squash them. The sensitive ones among us need a little more encouragement to produce their beautiful work.

Some of my quilting friends, on hearing this story, are initially disconcerted and ask, "Robyn, which do you think I am?" The truth is that I would not dare to make such a judgment; each of us knows which category fits us and that it may vary from time to time. The purpose of this story is not to label anyone, of course, but to encourage each of us to make the best of the personalities that she has been given.

I am writing this in mulberry season; I came in today like the child I once was with my hands and shirt covered in brilliant stain!

1992 Wild Berries
These are my quiting friends
198 cm x 198 cm

Workshop at "Quilt Experience", Minden

Celebrating with quilting friends